TEXAS

RICHARD RAMBECK

THE HISTORY OF THE

RANGERS

CREATIVE EDUCATION

8475030

Published by Creative Education
123 South Broad Street, Mankato, Minnesota 56001
Creative Education is an imprint of The Creative Company

Designed by Rita Marshall
Editorial assistance by Rosemary Wallner & John Nichols

Photos by: Allsport Photography, Focus on Sports, Fotosport,
SportsChrome.

Library of Congress Cataloging-in-Publication Data

Rambeck, Richard.
The History of the Texas Rangers / by Richard Rambeck.
p. cm. — (Baseball)
Summary: A team history of the Texas Rangers, resident of the Dallas–Fort
Worth area since 1972.
ISBN: 0-88682-927-5

1. Texas Rangers (Baseball team)—History—Juvenile literature.
[1. Texas Rangers (Baseball team)—History. 2. Baseball—History.]
I. Title. II. Series: Baseball (Mankato, Minn.)

GV875.T4R36   1999
796.357'64'09764531—dc21   97-9230

First edition

9 8 7 6 5 4 3 2 1

Texas natives say that everything is big in their state, and the biggest thing about the Dallas–Fort Worth region has been its growth. In 1900, fewer than 70,000 people resided in the area. By 1960, the population had grown to more than one million. At that time, professional sports leagues began taking an interest in establishing teams in the northeastern part of Texas—and in 1972, the Dallas–Fort Worth area got major league baseball's Texas Rangers.

The Rangers franchise moved to Texas after spending 11 mostly losing seasons in the U.S. capital, Washington, D.C. The team, then called the Senators, started out in Washing-

Mike Epstein of the Washington Senators.

Frank Howard smashed a team-record 48 home runs for the Washington Senators.

ton in 1961 as an expansion franchise in the American League. By the late 1960s, the Senators desperately needed to turn their fortunes around, and they nearly did by hiring former Boston Red Sox great Ted Williams as the team manager in 1969.

Williams managed to harness the hitting power of such Senators sluggers as Frank Howard, Mike Epstein, and Hank Allen in 1969. Howard hit .296 and slammed 48 homers. Epstein, a first baseman who had a terrible year at the plate in 1968, rebounded to hit 30 home runs in 1969.

Suddenly the lowly Senators, who had finished 31 games below .500 in 1968, jumped to 10 games over .500 in 1969. Attendance doubled at Washington home games as the Senators finished just one game out of third place. The team's improvement earned Williams the American League Manager of the Year award.

Unfortunately for Washington fans, the improvement didn't last. The Senators slumped to sixth place in the East Division of the American League in 1970 and were fifth in 1971. After that season, owner Robert Short announced he was moving the team west to Texas. The team, which changed its name to the Rangers, was going to play its home games in Arlington, a growing community about 20 miles from Dallas. There was already a stadium in Arlington, but it was hardly major-league quality. Soon, however, the 10,000-seat structure was expanded to 35,000 seats, and it was ready for the opening of the 1972 season.

Rangers star outfielder Rusty Greer.

1 9 7 2

Pitcher Dick Bosman lost the Rangers' first road game and won their first game in Arlington.

Ted Williams was still the team's manager, but his magic had apparently worn off. The Rangers were big losers again in 1972, and Williams retired after the season. The first Rangers team was bad, but the club soon improved behind new manager Whitey Herzog and then his replacement, Billy Martin. One major reason for the improvement was shortstop Toby Harrah.

Harrah was one of the few Texas Rangers who had spent a lot of time as a Washington Senator. In fact, he joined the Senators' organization in 1967 when he was traded by the Philadelphia Phillies. Harrah became the Senators' starting shortstop in 1971 when he was only 22 years old. He may have been one of the team's youngest starters, but in attitude he was wise beyond his years. "Ballplayers are like overgrown kids," he said. "We've played games all of our lives. We've been put above ordinary people by the fans. People write about us and give us things. It's easy to lose your perspective in this sort of life. But it's such a short part of our lives that we must try to enjoy it while we have it. That's what I'm determined to do—just get the most out of it."

The Rangers and their fans were convinced they were getting the most out of Harrah, who made up for what he lacked in natural ability by working harder than most players. "He's a complete ballplayer," said Martin. "He's a real battler." Harrah also had the respect of rival players and coaches. "Toby Harrah, in my opinion, handles the ball as well as any man in either league," said Cleveland manager Dave Garcia.

Harrah handled the ball and the bat well in 1974, but he was hardly the only story for the Rangers, who wound up second in the powerful American League West Division behind eventual World Series champion Oakland. (When the Rangers franchise moved from Washington to Texas, the team was moved from the American League East to the American League West.) Pitcher Ferguson Jenkins, who joined the club in 1973 after several outstanding seasons with the Chicago Cubs, compiled a 25–12 record in 1974, a victory total that still stands as a franchise all-time high. Power-hitting Jeff Burroughs blasted 25 home runs, drove in a league-leading 118 runs, and was named the American League Most Valuable Player.

1 9 7 4

Ferguson Jenkins pitched 29 complete games, setting a new Rangers record.

HARGROVE MAKES A BIG SPLASH AS A ROOKIE

Jeff Burroughs and Ferguson Jenkins had great years, but both would soon be traded. The player who had a great year in 1974 and would have the most lasting impact on the franchise was Mike Hargrove, a rookie first baseman. Hargrove, a native Texan, never expected to grow up to be a baseball player. His two best sports in high school were football and basketball. Like a lot of Texas boys, he loved football the most, but injuries he suffered in high school caused many colleges to lose interest in him as a football player. As a result, Hargrove went to tiny Northwestern Oklahoma State University in Alva on a basketball scholarship.

Hargrove was a good basketball player, but he wasn't pro material. His father suggested he try out for baseball, but Hargrove wasn't sure the diamond game was for him. "I

Knuckleballer Charlie Hough.

Infielder Toby Harrah. 11

didn't want to embarrass myself," he said. "I didn't know how good I would be." He turned out to be very good—so good, in fact, that some pro scouts told Hargrove he would be chosen in the early rounds of the 1972 amateur draft. Unfortunately for Hargrove, the scouts had been too optimistic. He wasn't selected until the 25th round when the Texas Rangers drafted him.

Al Oliver had an outstanding year, leading Texas with a .324 average and driving in 89 runs.

Hargrove spent the rest of the 1972 season in the Rangers' minor-league system. At first, he didn't hit well—actually, he hardly hit at all—and he was ready to hang up his spikes and try something else. But he didn't, and it was largely because of his father. "As a kid, Dad had always wanted to play ball himself, but he missed his chances to try out," Hargrove said of his father. "Once he had pneumonia, and an-

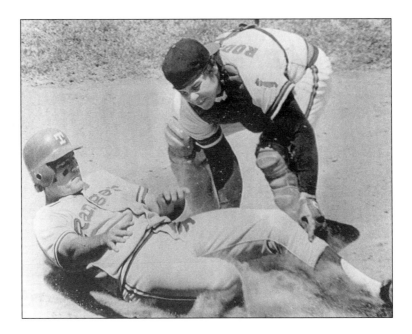

Rangers standout, Mike Hargrove.

other time he had to stay home to harvest." Unlike his father, Mike Hargrove hadn't missed his chance to try out, and he was determined to make the most of it.

Hargrove improved rapidly during the 1973 season, and when he reported to spring training in 1974, Rangers manager Billy Martin had plans for the young first baseman—major-league plans. "I'm putting you on the team," Martin told Hargrove just before the 1974 season. "If you don't like the idea, I can change my mind." Hargrove not only liked the idea, he responded by batting .323 in 1974, which was good enough to earn him the American League Rookie of the Year award.

Fleet-footed Bump Wills led Texas in stolen bases (35) for the third season in a row.

The young Ranger had become a star almost overnight, but he wasn't about to let it go to his head. "Mike has not changed one bit since the first day," explained Toby Harrah, Hargrove's best friend on the team. "That's something you don't often see in someone as successful as he has been." Nor was Hargrove one to complain if things weren't going his way. During the 1975 season, Martin played him in the outfield, although Hargrove believed his best position was first base. But Hargrove headed to the outfield without arguing with his manager about the occasional position switch. "I don't figure I've been here long enough to talk to him [Martin] about it," Hargrove reasoned. "He's doing what he thinks is best for myself and the team."

Martin guided the Rangers to a winning season in 1975, but then left to manage the New York Yankees. The Rangers' new skipper, Frank Lucchesi, inherited a club with a number of young, quality hitters—Hargrove, Harrah, Burroughs, and Roy Smalley—and several veteran pitchers, including Jim

Along with fellow Ranger Jim Sundberg, third baseman Buddy Bell won a Gold Glove award for his fine defensive play.

Bibby and Gaylord Perry. It was a club that wasn't expected to do much but soon jumped into contention for the American League West title. "We're still a hungry team," Harrah explained. "Except for the pitchers, most of us haven't been around long enough to get involved in too many other things, so we spend a lot of time together. It's not quite like the old days when the players traveled on trains, but a lot of us live in Texas all year, and we hang around together."

Unfortunately for this young band of Rangers, the team, despite its talent, wasn't able to capture first place. Between 1976 and 1981, the Rangers never finished lower than fourth in the American League West, but they couldn't overcome the superior talent of the Kansas City Royals and the Oakland Athletics. The Texas fans, who had seen their team rise to the level of contender and then not improve much, began to take it out on some of the veterans—and nobody heard more boos than Harrah, who had given the Rangers several years of steady play. Finally, after the 1978 season, the team traded Harrah to the Cleveland Indians for another third baseman, Buddy Bell. "Every day you could just open the paper and read about how bad Toby was," Hargrove recalled. "The treatment he received from the press was terrible."

BELL RINGS IN SEVERAL GOOD SEASONS

Toby Harrah's replacement was a player who had grown up around baseball. Buddy Bell's father, Gus, played in the majors from 1950 to 1964 for four teams. Bell knew early on that he wanted to follow in his father's footsteps. "I never wanted to do anything but be an athlete," Bell said. "More

Second baseman Julio Franco made all the tough plays.

The powerful Jeff Burroughs.

than anything else I enjoy the fun. It's not so much on the field, but before and after the game. We're still kids. People come off the street and ask themselves, 'Are these guys 30 [years old] or 10?' But I think you should stay as young as you can for as long as you can."

Bell used that attitude to stay as consistent as any Ranger has been in club history. In his first four years in Texas, Bell batted .304 and won the Gold Glove fielding award all four seasons. Bell made hitting and fielding look easy, and he believed he achieved his success because he didn't try to make things difficult. "I'm probably one of the least scientific players of all time," he admitted. "If you think too much, you make the game too complicated. You hit the ball and catch the ball, and that's about it. When I go to [off-season baseball] clinics, the other instructors don't think I'm very bright."

Bell immediately became one of the cornerstones of the Rangers' team. In fact, he may have been *the* cornerstone. "He's the guy I'd build a franchise around," said Texas relief pitcher Jim Kern. "Defensively, he's an interesting combination of [New York Yankees third baseman] Graig Nettles and [Detroit Tigers third baseman] Aurelio Rodriguez. He has Nettles's reactions and range and Rodriguez's arm." But despite his fielding and batting heroics, Bell didn't have the reputation of a top star. He just quietly put together one quality season after another. Kern had a theory about why Bell wasn't given his due as a star. "It's partly because he's played for mediocre teams in parks that aren't great for hitters, but I think the main reason is that he's so smooth he makes everything look simple."

Bell made a lot of things look simple in 1980. In addition

1 9 8 3

Rick Honeycutt's league-leading 2.42 ERA earned him a spot on the AL All-Star team.

Ruben Sierra: a tough Ranger (pages 18-19).

The Rangers, under new manager Bobby Valentine, set 49 team and individual records.

to winning the Gold Glove award, he batted .329, sixth-best in the American League, drove in 83 runs, and hit 17 homers. Bell had another good year in 1981, as the Rangers wound up second in the division. Hopes were high for 1982, but the club fell apart, finishing in last place with a 64–98 record. Manager Don Zimmer was fired and eventually replaced by Doug Rader, who said, "We've got our work cut out for us." The Rangers knew they had to make major changes, which meant that any player could be traded—including Bell—if it might help the club.

Bell stayed in Texas, however, and in 1983 he rewarded Rangers management with a productive year in the field and at the plate. But in July 1985, the Rangers finally said goodbye to the consistent Bell, trading him to the Cincinnati Reds. For Bell the trade was a bittersweet moment. He was going home to the city of his birth and was leaving a last-place team for a club with a legitimate chance to win the pennant. But Bell still cried as he bid farewell to his Texas teammates and to an organization he had served well for nearly seven seasons.

RANGERS ROOKIES COME TOGETHER AS A TEAM

Without Buddy Bell and a solid cast of veteran players, the Rangers' new manager, Bobby Valentine, was forced to build his first team, in 1986, around 10 rookies. One of them, outfielder Pete Incaviglia, hit 30 home runs. Another rookie, pitcher Edwin Correa, notched 12 victories and 189 strikeouts. A third, pitcher Bobby Witt, had 11 wins and 174 strikeouts. And a fourth rookie, relief pitcher Mitch Williams, made 80 appearances in one season, a major-league record for rookies. But Valentine insisted that the Rangers' season, in which the team led the division for 46 days before falling to second and staying there, was a team effort.

"This was a team by the true definition of the word," Valentine said. "It was a team that believed in itself and in each other. It believed in what we were trying to do as a group. . . . We never said we would sacrifice winning for anything. If I did things early that might have sacrificed a game, it was because I believed it would produce more wins later on. Everything was focused on winning."

The newly acquired Julio Franco was named to the AL All-Star team along with teammate Ruben Sierra.

Unfortunately, the Rangers soon lost that focus. The team slumped to last place again in 1987, but later showed steady improvement. The 1989 season produced an 83–79 record, which was good enough to earn the Rangers fourth place in the powerful American League West. Their success was keyed by the hitting of outfielder Ruben Sierra (.306 average, 29 home runs, and 119 RBIs) and infielder Julio Franco (.316, 13 home runs, and 92 RBIs). There were also strong pitching performances from youngsters Kevin Brown (12–9, 3.35 ERA) and Witt (12–13), as well as from veteran Nolan Ryan (16–10, 3.20 ERA), who was signed as a free agent before the 1989 season.

Nolan Ryan's outstanding year attracted a lot of media attention, which might have prevented some fans from knowing just how good Sierra, the 24-year-old right fielder, was in 1989. Many baseball experts thought Sierra, not Milwaukee Brewers center fielder Robin Yount, should have won the American League Most Valuable Player award. The confident Sierra felt the same way. "I led the league in RBIs, total

Promising young left-hander Darren Oliver.

bases, slugging percentage, extra-base hits, and triples," Sierra said. "And I was there in all the major [hitting] categories. He [Yount] beat me in batting average and doubles." Sierra was so confident he was going to capture the MVP trophy that he picked a spot for it on top of his television set back home in his native Puerto Rico. "I was so sure," he said. But the award went to Yount.

First baseman Rafael Palmeiro slugged 49 doubles to lead the league and set the Rangers' record.

RANGERS BUILD A WINNING CHEMISTRY

In both the 1990 and 1991 seasons, the Rangers finished in third place. Nolan Ryan continued his solid pitching. On May 1, 1991, he threw his seventh career no-hitter in a 3–0 win over the Toronto Blue Jays. At 44 years old that year, he became the oldest pitcher in history to throw a no-hitter. In 1993, Ryan, the all-time strikeout leader, retired from baseball. In his long career, Ryan notched 5,714 strikeouts—1,578 more than his nearest competition.

In 1994, the Rangers enjoyed some firsts. The team played its first game in a new state-of-the-art stadium, The Ballpark in Arlington. In August of that year, in a game against the California Angels, pitcher Kenny Rogers became the first Rangers pitcher ever to throw a perfect game—the Angels were held without a base-runner the entire game. By midseason, the Rangers led the AL West. Unfortunately, a players' strike cut the season short, and the Rangers ended up with a record of 52–62. The losing season was a disappointment to the organization, and manager Kevin Kennedy was fired.

In October of 1994, former big-league catcher Johnny Oates was named the Rangers' new manager. Oates took a look at his new team's roster and liked what he saw. Out-fielder Juan Gonzalez had joined the team in 1991 and had blossomed into one of baseball's most feared sluggers. By 1995, the 26-year-old native of Puerto Rico had already led the American League in home runs twice. "'Igor' [Gonzalez] is unbelievably strong, and yet he has such quick hands," noted teammate Dean Palmer. "Even when he gets fooled [by a pitch] he can recover and then just snap his wrists—the ball goes 450 feet."

The Rangers also featured catcher Ivan Rodriguez. Nick-named "Pudge" by his teammates, the stocky Rodriguez was immediately recognized as one of the top defensive catchers in baseball. After joining the Rangers as a 19-year-old rookie in 1991, Pudge's extraordinarily quick feet and

1 9 9 4

Designated hitter Jose Canseco socked 31 home runs and drove in 90 runs to lead the Rangers' club.

Rangers ace closer Jeff Russell.

bazooka throwing arm quickly earned him the respect of all opposing base-stealers. By 1995, Rodriguez had also blossomed offensively; his .298 average with 16 home runs in 1994 proved he had arrived as a hitter. The Rangers also signed free agent first baseman Will Clark to provide extra pop in the middle of the lineup and to add veteran leadership. Clark had been a five-time National League All-Star for the San Francisco Giants and had also won a Gold Glove award for his fielding. "We've got some young guys, and we've got some veterans, like Will, who've been through the wars," said Oates. "We'll need them all if we expect to go anywhere."

Kenny Rogers pitched 39 consecutive scoreless innings to set the club record.

By 1995 Oates had become used to his new team of players. The Rangers finished with a 74–70 record that year—a third-place finish. But the 1996 season would surpass all others. The Rangers started 1996 by winning their first seven games. Gonzalez and third baseman Palmer became a powerful hitting duo. By the beginning of June, the Rangers had sizzled to a 34–19 start. Texas cooled somewhat during the next two months, but by August the club was back on top. Gonzalez, Rodriguez, and outfielder Rusty Greer were unstoppable, pushing the team to new heights on the field and in the standings.

By September, the Rangers found themselves all alone in first place in the AL West. The 25-year-old franchise went on to capture its first-ever division championship. "It's been a long time coming," said a smiling Oates. "I feel very happy for our fans."

The Rangers now faced the New York Yankees in their first-ever postseason game. Although the Rangers won the

Fastest gun in the AL West, catcher Ivan Rodriguez (pages 26-27).

first game, they lost the next three. The Yankees took the division title and went on to win the World Series.

Texas hadn't won the series, but Rangers players and staff were honored with other rewards. Juan Gonzalez, who homered in all four games against the Yankees, was named the 1996 American League Most Valuable Player. Oates was named Co-Manager of the Year. At the age of 24, Rodriguez won his fifth-straight Gold Glove award for catching. He had thrown out 49 percent of all base-runners attempting to steal, leading the majors for the second year in a row.

Defensively, the club had a nearly perfect season. Rangers fielders committed only 87 errors—the fewest in club history. They also played 15 games in a row with no errors. "That's the thing I'm most proud of," said Oates.

1 9 9 6

The Rangers retired Nolan Ryan's number 34 on September 15. The 300-game winner is the only Ranger to be so honored.

KEEPING THE WINNING SPIRIT

In 1997, the Rangers celebrated their first 25 years of baseball in the Dallas–Fort Worth area. They also added more major-league muscle to their team. Yankees pitcher John Wetteland, the MVP of the 1996 World Series, signed on as a free agent with the Rangers in 1997. "He's the piece of the puzzle we needed to get to the next level," said Texas general manager Doug Melvin. Also signed was infielder Billy Ripken, brother of Baltimore Orioles great Cal Ripken. They joined Ivan Rodriguez, Juan Gonzalez, pitcher Roger Pavlik, the reliable Rusty Greer, and first baseman Will Clark to form the core of what many experts thought would be a formidable playoff team in 1997.

"We have an experienced team that we feel can go a long way," said Melvin at the beginning of the season. But then a rash of serious injuries decimated the team. Before the season, Juan Gonzalez tore ligaments in his thumb while playing winter baseball in Puerto Rico. By August, steady second baseman Mark McLemore was out with a damaged left knee, and Pavlik was out with an injury to his elbow. Clark was on the injured list five times—with injuries to his heel, wrist, right calf, ribs, and thigh.

1 9 9 8

The Rangers were looking for a lot of saves from hard-throwing 1996 World Series MVP Jim Wetteland.

With all the hurt players, the team couldn't match their winning 1996 season. "If we stand around waiting for Will and Juan to come back," said a worried Johnny Oates, "we'll be in big trouble."

The injuries didn't last forever, though. A recovered Gonzalez came back to launch 42 homers and drive in 130 RBIs. "He's the best RBI player I've ever seen," admired Oates.

Despite Gonzalez's surge, the Rangers were 10 games out of first place by the end of August. The team had made more errors than they had during all of the previous season. During one game, a television camera caught Oates burying his face in his hands. "I hope this isn't what can be expected," said a frustrated Oates. "We'll go to work every day and do the best we can."

The Rangers ended the season with a solid 77–85 record, good enough for third place. "We're not satisfied with our record," remarked Oates. "But I am happy that our guys never gave up, considering our injury problems."

Texas looks to use that determination to push their way back into the postseason hunt. With a lineup that features

One of baseball's most feared sluggers, Juan Gonzalez.

Hardworking second baseman Mark McLemore. 31

such players as Greer, McLemore, Gonzalez, Clark, and Rodriguez, it appears injuries would be the only thing that could slow down the Rangers' attack.

On the defensive side, Texas will count on a starting rotation of John Burkett, Darren Oliver, Bobby Witt, and Aaron Sele to stifle opposing hitters, while Rodriguez's strong right arm should once again keep the league's base-stealers in check. Closer John Wetteland continues to be one of the game's premier late-inning stoppers, and Oates has emerged as a top-flight skipper. "We have yet to see this team's best baseball," noted Melvin. "If we can stay healthy and our pitching holds, we will be a factor in any race."

In the state of Texas, where bigger is always better, it would only be fitting that the Rangers someday take home baseball's biggest prize: a World Series championship.